Foreign Direct Investment in Hungary between 1990 and 1995

By Sebastian Meyer

Digital Edition

Copyright © 2010 Sebastian Meyer

All Rights Reserved

Table of Contents

I. Hungary's macroeconomic status in the early 90s ... 1

II. Definition of FDI in comparison to Portfolio Investment 3

   1.) Evaluation of inflows between 1990 and 1995 ... 4

   2.) Case: Schöller Lebensmittel GmbH & Co. KG .. 7

III. Conclusion 9

IV. Appendix 10

V. References 25

I. Hungary's macroeconomic status in the early 90s

How was it feasible that between 1990 and 1995 Hungary was the most successful and the first East and Central European transition nation in decoying Foreign Direct Investment (FDI) of Western firms (Table 1) even though its overall macroeconomic performance suffered amongst others from the transition recession which was as dramatic as the output decline of the Great Depression between 1930 and 1934? (Table 2.1 and 2.2). Moreover its economic growth was characterized as less competitive compared to a Western nation resulting from a low production and aggregated demand as well as grave foreign and domestic imbalances? It faced a high level of inherited foreign debt due to structural deficits of the former Soviet centrally planned regime.

They had a low amount of capital and technology as important factors of production. (Hunya, 1996: 3-6). For reducing this permanent debt, the Hungarian government consequently considered internal and external financing. Internal financing did not work efficiently because the Hungarian government as debtors could not receive enough remittances from the Hungarian public in the long term. (Table 3). The situation was fragile. The gross domestic product (GDP) including their real disposable income as well as confidence in their own economy and government was not high enough in the long run. To go a step further, the Hungarian government thus needed to persuade external debtors because it has more prospects to find potential investors.

This paper looks for explanations for this macroeconomic contradiction.

The Hungarian economic development in the early 90s greatly differed from other transition nations like the Czech Republic which had a more stable macroeconomic development (Table 4.1 and 4.2) but a weaker share of foreign direct investment in GDP than Hungary between 1990 and 1995. (Hunya, 1996: 11). (Table 5.1 and 5.2). Foreign investors were attracted to Hungary by the liberalization of market institutions and prices plus the adoption of flexible convertible foreign exchange rates as well as privatization through rapid exit of state-owned trading monopolies. (Gros and Steinherr, 2004: 61-77). Therefore, market share could easily be taken by the products of local subsidiaries of private international enterprises because the business sector was relatively independent on state intervention. The Hungarian government has opened up its economy to FDI investors since the mid 1980s because it had already had "joint venture" during the late Soviet regime. (Turnock, 2005: 9). ''More than 11,000 foreign joint ventures have been established in Hungary, with about 5,000 of them in 1991 alone.''(Gombocz, 1993: 2). Joint ventures are an equity investment where a separate organization is formed which had been disbursed for in part by Western money or which made "Western products" under license or patent. In sum, the Hungarian economy accepted more and more terms in privatization sales and trade activities because it regarded them, in contrast to Poland and Czech Republic, as a primary importance for its national budget and the balance of payment.

II. Definition of FDI in comparison to Portfolio Investment

I chose to discuss FDI using Hungary as an example because of its economic relevance shown in Graph. Particularly for transition nations like Hungary, the topic FDI has become an interesting and significant issue in global statistics since at least the beginning of 2000s. Interestingly, according to Guisinger et al. (2002), the worldwide flow of FDI increased by over ''1000%'' compared to world trade (91%) and world output (27%)[1].

FDI is a wholly equity based market entry participation strategy where foreign capital [cash] flows [of funding] like inter alia organizational assets and know how (Guisinger et al., 2003: 316) are provided by a cross border private firm investor to establish a foreign multinational company (Greenfield FDI) or finance an existing company that the investors owns (Acquisition) in the long run. Ownership and control are important because the investor has or acquires the power to have a substantial impact on the foreign company's value chain activities like finance management.

The share of the equity the investor has to own is 10%. (Eiteman et al., 2010, 84).

---

[1] WTO (1998). *World Trade Organization Annual Report, 1998.* New York: United Nations.

On one level, its advantages comprise lower costs of supplying the host country by avoiding tariffs and quotas. Next, a foreign domestic firm may have a greater opportunity to adapt product to local markets insuring a better local image of the product and after-market service.

On another level, as FDI includes an increased capital investment of managerial and other resources (drain or talent) implying cost of coordinating units as well as represents a greater exposure of the investment to political and financial risks, it is rather convenient for most experienced international firms.

In essence, FDI is a movement of capital across national borders in a manner that grants the investor control over the acquired asset. Thus, it is distinct from portfolio investment. On the contrary, it is capital invested in activities that expect a financial return rather than control or management of the investment. Eventually, its motivating forces are profits and risks.

1.) Evaluation of inflows between 1990 and 1995

In the following, I assess the level and pattern of FDI flows to Hungary between 1990 and 1995. I choose this time period because Hungary, which received considerable high cumulative financial inflows into its transitional economy during this period, was the most dynamic part compared to its neighboring Central and Eastern European Nations (CEEN). (Ingham, 2004: 123).

Table 6 reports the highest convergence in UN and OECD estimates of Hungarian FDI between 1989 and 1995. Since 1989 more than 80% of all FDI went inter alia to Hungary. (Gradev, 2001: 3). Thereafter, table 7 analyses the UN data in more detail. Ranked on a per capita basis, the dominant role of Hungary in attracting FDI is apparent. To dare a step further, table 8 sets out a comprehensive picture of FDI flows to Hungary. Subsequently, its success in maintaining continuing high levels of FDI flows is obvious - an achievement which continued into 1995. FDI flows to Hungary were low during 1990 and 1992, particularly in 1990 the first year of transition. This is not surprising, provided the risks and uncertainties resulting from "transition shocks", import and export competition and price liberalization for instance. Though in 1990 the Hungarian economy had already taken the initiative of liberalizing and privatizing market institutions and competitive prices, it failed to provide "immediate relief" to combat its existing budget deficit and debt under these new circumstances as soon as possible. But between 1990 and 1991, there was an abrupt increase of FDI inflows from about 350 ($m) to 1460 ($m).

Hungary had a better-prepared environment for foreign investors since about 90% of all imports were liberalized and the privatization policy favored cash sales to the highest bidder which was an advantage for western investors. Additionally, government policies implying general tax exemptions to foreign firms in 1990 also played a key role. (Hunya, 1996: 8). Hence, we had new incentives for FDI resulting in a higher FDI inflow between 1990 and 1991. Between 1992 and 1994, when Hungary received about 1479 ($m) in 1992, 2350 ($m) in 1993 and 1510 ($m) in 1994, its uniquely high degree of FDI penetration was ranked among the first five net capital importing countries agreeable to Gabor Hunya. Consequently, there was a tremendously high degree of privatization of many enterprises from Western investors. Thereby, new private companies replaced the production of state-owned enterprises (SOE). Subsequently, many domestic enterprises collapsed due to the establishment of free markets and the abandonment of the state-public monopoly. Hungary also encountered a rise in unemployment. This macroeconomic problem was resolved through a "consolidation program" with subsidized credit schemes for domestic and local investors carried out during 1993 and 1994. To sum up, SOE could only really survive by inviting more foreign investors. Thus, since mid-1993, FDI in the Hungarian economy was rising. By 1995, FDI flows match the maximum with about 4500 ($m) in Hungary. Thence, we also had higher growth-rates in the industrial sector: Manufacturing production equaled 30,63 US $m and engineering 22,94 US $m for instance. (Table 9). Next, Hungarian government policies favored even more FDI including lower profits tax for reinvested profits in 1995 and negotiable individual tax exemptions for large Western investors. Another comparative advantage over Poland and Czech Republic was the strong presence of major multinational enterprises (Moosa, 2002: 6-11) with cheap labor cost compared to western locations. But why do we observe a substantial decline of FDI inflows from 1995 and 1996?

Firstly, the inflow of FDI and the speed of privatization slowed down in 1995. Foreign investors perceived more and more economic uncertainties related to the inflation rate. It accelerated from about 18% to 28% in 1995 due to currency devaluation and the (private) price increase for public services. (Hunya, 1996: 6). Hence, "Greenfield or joint venture investors" hesitated or rejected new profitable offers and attractive projects. There was a slow-down of privatization. As already mentioned beforehand, in 1994, privatization policy changed in favor of domestic and local investors. Finally, Hungary lost its comparative advantages over other CEEN since no further stimulus for FDI was introduced for maintaining the 5 ($m) maximum beyond 1995.

2.) Case: Schöller Lebensmittel GmbH & Co. KG

The main Western investor contributing to the FDI dynamism in the early 90s was the German frozen food and ice cream manufacturer Schöller. (Table 10). I chose this sector because, by 1995, with about 30,63 US $m it was the strongest one and Schöller was the first major ice cream producer investing in the Hungarian food market. (Estrin, Hughes, Todd, 1997: 130). Until

nowadays, Germany remains the main FDI investors with 25% of all FDI. (Graph 2). What was its motivation and behavior?

First of all, Schöller was mainly attracted by the liberalization of FDI and prices and the existing deficiencies of Hungary's retail services inherited from the socialist economy of shortage. (Turnock, 2005: 269). Subsequently, it looked for new market share opportunities including inter alia the location and market size hypothesis. Low real wages were one locational advantage. Thus Hungary, which offered cheap labor compared to western locations, attracted labor intensive production like ice cream and frozen food manufacturing from a relatively high wage country like Germany. In conclusion, the ''Hungarian cheap labor hypothesis'' also proves Love and Lage – Hidalgo statement implying that real labor cost differences between a developed nation and an emerging country have a considerable effect on the flow of FDI. (Love and Lage – Hidalgo, 2000:1259-67). (Table 11). Thereby, Schöller increased the employment rate, stabilized its sales productivity through cheaper capital cost, superior management and technology in form of advanced entrepreneurial and operation efficiency. Furthermore, it aimed for a perfect market share opportunity. Minding economies of scale, it concentrated on one market segment allowing for specialization in frozen food and ice cream and hence production cost minimization. Finally, the goal was to manufacture for the Hungarian ice cream and food market whilst expanding and diversifying its market segment globally. A further factor of attraction was the dominant presence of a ''suitable'' milk manufacturer called Budatej it established a joint venture – Schöller - Budatej with. (Estrin et al., 1997 : 135f.). In essence, it focused on a non-transferable expertise konwledge and brand reputation as well as avoiding tarrifs/ quotas and considering '' profitable'' exchange rates.

III. Conclusion

This paper examined how FDI was essential in ameliorating e.g. Hungary's weakly developed manufacturing sector for frozen food and ice cream. I agree to the statement that, on the one hand, '' FDI [from Western investors] can be regarded as a 'New Marshall Plan' to help [Hungary]''(Gowan, 1995: 10) through which superior capital and labour management, technology and market research comprising promotion, advertising and network distribution have improved the Hungarian aggregated output in the food and ice cream manufacturing sector in the early 90s.

On the other hand, I disagree with this statement as it is applicable in the short run only. Following a record year in 1995, FDI inflows began to gradually decline. (Table 12). Ultimately, it took Hungary another six years to reverse this trend. Thus, FDI inflows cannot be seen as a permanent one way investment.

Finally, in my view FDI can merely be regarded as a short term 'New Marshall Plan' as FDI in – and outflows are depended upon macroeconomic variables like exchange rate (regimes), interest rate policies by the Hungarian central bank, balance of payments and inflation rate.

IV. Appendix

Table 1:

FDI inflows into CEE (Central Eastern Europe), 1990-1995 ($ mln)

	1990-95 Average
Albania	42
Belarus	12
Bosnia & Hercegovina	–
Bulgaria	57
Croatia	120
Czech Republic	947
Estonia	165
Hungary	1863
Latvia	116
Lithuania	36
Macedonia	17
Moldova	31
Poland	1396
Romania	162
Russia	1167
Serbia & Montenegro	82
Slovakia	147
Slovenia	100
Ukraine	206
Total	6666*

Source: UNCTAD (2002) pp.305-6.
Note * excludes Bosnia and Hercegovina

Table 2.1:

How did transition economies perform?

The Transition Recession			
Countries	Consecutive years of output decline	Cumulative output decline (percent)	Real GDP, 2000 (1990 = 100)
CSB[a]	3.8	22.6	106.5
Albania	3	33	110
Bulgaria	4	16	81
Croatia	4	36	87
Czech Republic	3	12	99
Estonia	5	35	85
Hungary	4	15	109
Latvia	6	51	61
Lithuania	5	44	67
Poland	2	6	112
Romania	3	21	144
Slovak Republic	4	23	82
Slovenia	3	14	105

Source: http://siteresources.worldbank.org/INTECA/Resources/part1.pdf [accessed on 05.03.2010].

Table 2.2:

Comparison of output decline during the Great Depression 1930 – 1934 with USA, UK and F

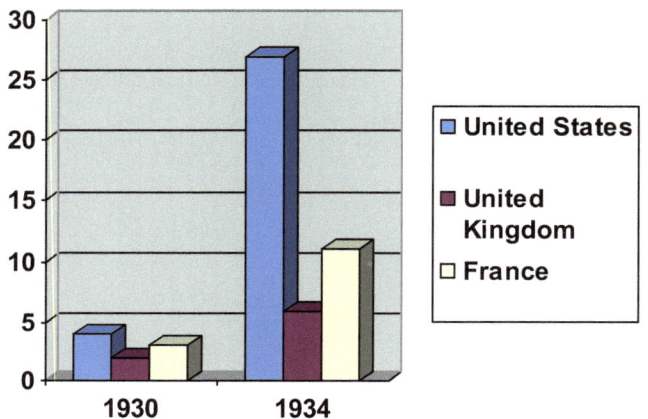

Source: http://www.worldbank.org/html/prddr/trans/janfeb95/pgs17-18.htm [accessed on 6.3.10]

Table 3:

Gross debt per capita (in USD) – A comparison between Czech Republic and Hungary in 1990

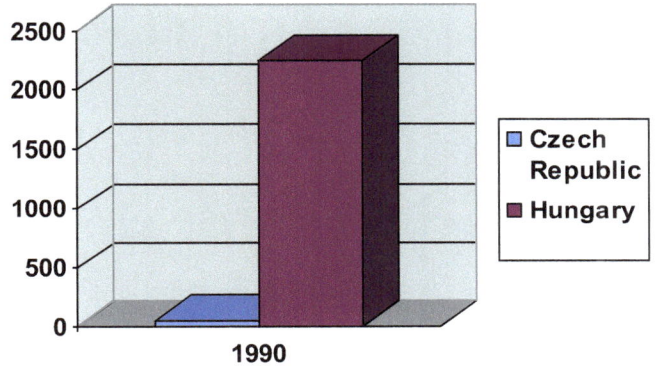

Source: WIIW Handbook of Statistics (1997), p. 45.

Table 4.1:

Countries in transition in 1990 – A comparison between Czech Republic and Hungary in 1990

Real growth rates (in %) of	Hungary	Czech Republic
Gross domestic product	-3,5	-1,2
Gross industrial production	-10,2	-3,3
Gross agriculture production	-4,8	-2,3

Source: WIIW Handbook of Statistics (1997), p. 46.

Table 4.2:

Countries in transition: Consumer prices (GDP deflator) (annual % average)

Countries	1989
Czechoslovakia	1,4
Hungary	17,0
Poland	251,1

Source: IMF, World Economic Outlook.

Table 5.1:

Inward FDI stock as a percentage of GDP in CEE

Country/region	1995
World average	10.0
CEE average	5.4
Albania	8.7
Belarus	0.5
Bosnia and Hercegovina	1.1
Bulgaria	3.4
Croatia	2.5
Czech Republic	14.1
Estonia	14.1
Hungary	26.7
Latvia	12.5
Lithuania	5.8
Macedonia	0.7
Moldova	6.5
Poland	6.2
Romania	3.2
Russia	1.6
Serbia and Montenegro	2.7
Slovakia	4.4
Slovenia	9.4
Ukraine	2.5

Source: United Nations (2003) p.3.

Table 5.2:

FDI stock as a percentage of gross domestic product, 1990-1995 in Hungary (in percent)

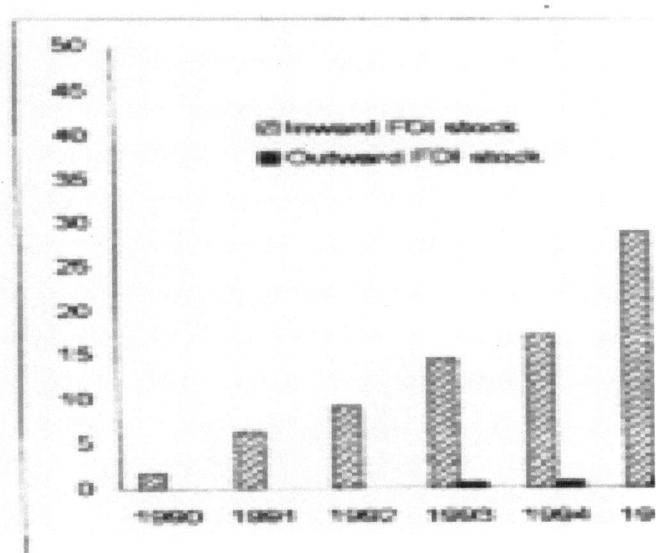

Source: UNCTAD (2001), p.2.

Graph 1:

Globalization: Growth of Foreign Direct Investment Inflows ($Bil) 1980-2008

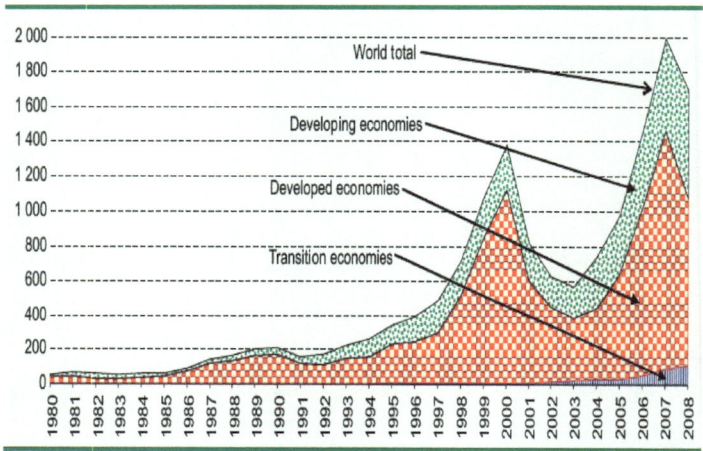

Source: UNCTAD FDI/TNC database (www.unctad.org/fdistatistics) and UNCTAD Secretariat estimates.

Table 6:

Cumulative flows of FDI to CEE, 1995 estimates

Host countries	1989–95, cumulative, $bn Data sources	
	UN[a] 1989–95	OECD 1989–1995/Q2
Czech Republic	5.6	3.4
Hungary	11.2	9.9
Poland	n/a	3.9
CEE 10	n/a	22.3
Russian Federation	5.5	3.3
Total: CEE and CIS	n/a	27.9

[a] 1994: UN estimates; 1995/Q2 = second quarter of 1995.

Sources: UN World Investment Report (1996), Geneva: United Nations, reported in Financial Times, 17 July 1996; OECD unpublished estimates (1996).

Table 7:

FDI inflows to four largest recipients, CEE and the CIS, 1989 -94

	Cumulative flows	%	Per capita
Czech Republic	3,102	14.9	301.1
Hungary	6,801	32.7	660.2
Poland	4,184	20.1	108.9
CEE 10	16,870	81.2	159.9
Russian Federation	2,300	11.0	15.5
Other	1,585	7.6	n/a
Total	20,755	100.0	n/a

[a]1994: UN estimates.

Source: *UN World Investment Report* (1995), Geneva: United Nations.

Table 8:

FDI flows to Hungary 1990-1997 $ (mln)

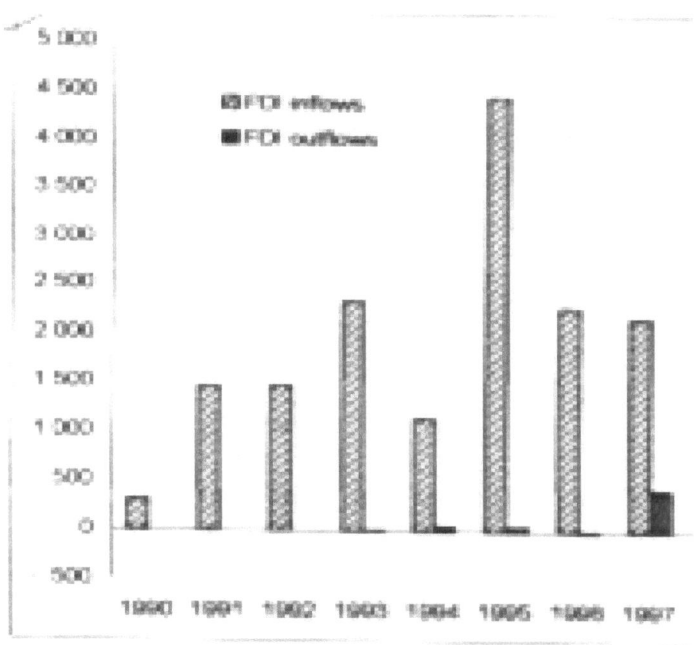

Source: UNCTAD (2001), p.1.

Table 9:

Sector breakdown of FDI into Hungary, January – July 1995

Sector	US $mln	% of total
Agriculture	2,62	2,7
Mining	**1,46**	**1,5**
Manufacturing	30,63	31,5
Construction	**21,30**	**21**
Others	41,04	42,13
Total	**97,05**	**100,00**

Source: KSH, Havi Közlemények (monthly reports) 1995/6

Table 10:

Distribution of cases by sector and host country

Sector	Czech Republic	Hungary
Food and drink (low technolgy)		Nestlé Schöller
Pharma (high technolgy)	gsk GlaxoSmithKline	
Engineering (medium technology)	OTIS	LYCETT BEER & ALE
Glass (low technology)		GUARDIAN

Source: Estrin, S., 1997, *Foreign Direct Investment in Central and Eastern Europe – Multinationals in Transition*, Royal Institute of International Affaires, London, First Edition: 63.

Table 11:

Sales and employment in Schöller – Budatej

	1990	1991	1992	1993	1994
Sales (HUF'000s)	**1,191,715**	715,345	**2,142,994**	2,403,256	**2,995,356**
Employment	**264**	286	**328**	357	**392**

Source: Source: Estrin, S., 1997, *Foreign Direct Investment in Central and Eastern Europe – Multinationals in Transition*, Royal Institute of International Affaires, London, First Edition: 136.

V. References

Eitman, D. et al., 2010, *Multinational Business Finance,* Pearson, Boston, Twelfth Edition.

Estrin, S. et al., 1997, *Foreign Direct Investment in Central and Eastern Europe – Multinationals in Transition*, Royal Institute of International Affaires, London, First Edition.

Hunya. G., 1996, *Foreign Direct Investment in Hungary: A key Elementof Economic modernization,* The
Vienna Institute for comparative economic studies (WIIW) no. 226.

Gombocz, Z., 1993, *Business Guide to Hungary,* Budapest.

Gowan, P., 1995, *Neo-Liberal Theory and Practices for Eastern Europe*, New Left Review no. 213.

Gradev, G., 2001, *EU Companies in eastern Europe: Strategic Choices and Labour effects,* in G. Gradev (ed), *CEE Countries in EU: Companies' Strategies of Industrial Restructuring and Relocation,* European Trade Union Institute, Brussels.

Gros, D. et al., 2004, *Economic Transition in Central and Eastern Europe – Planting the Seeds,* Cambridge University Press, New York, Second Edition.

Ingham, B., 2004, *International Economics – A European Focus*, FT Prentice Hall, London.

Love, J.H. and Lage-Hidalgo, F., 2000, *Analysing the determinants of US direct investment in Mexico,* Applied economics no. 32.

Moosa, I., 2002, *Foreign Direct Investment – Theory, Evidence and Practice*, Palgrave Macmilan, London.

Turnock, D., 2005, *Foreign Direct Investment and Regional Development in East Central Europe and the former Soviet*

Union, Ashgate Economic Geography Series, University of Leicester, UK, first Edition.

.

www.ingramcontent.com/pod-product-compliance
Lightning Source LLC
Chambersburg PA
CBHW040347220526
45473CB00009B/2810